Liberia, a Bulwark of Rage

Liberia, a Bulwark of Rage
My First Home

Lawrence D. Taplah

authorHOUSE®

AuthorHouse™
1663 Liberty Drive
Bloomington, IN 47403
www.authorhouse.com
Phone: 1 (800) 839-8640

Published by AuthorHouse 06/18/2015

ISBN: 978-1-5049-1764-3 (sc)
ISBN: 978-1-5049-1763-6 (e)

Library of Congress Control Number: 2015909435

Print information available on the last page.

INTRODUCTION

Should Liberians accept their social condition for existence by racial profiling? Yes, I believe so. Liberians do not know what makes them racist and they cannot point to anything for this belief. That which arouses racial profiling among Liberians is to deny the interlocking system of group thinking, which has become nothing but an illusion and a myth. This book is about the revelation of racial profiling in Liberia. While reading this book you will be exposed to the accusatory writings of Liberians and non-Liberians about racial profiling. To read my assertion that racial profiling exists between two groups of Liberians is the ultimate reason for this book. Racial profiling is close to being oppressive and stifling. But, it is also a disclosure to identify one's self in a group. It can be used as a bulwark of rage to clarify the social condition of Liberians.

This realization of using racial profiling is a distinctive way for Liberians to form customs, practices and laws that are used to keep an identity. Do you want to take this journey with me? Racial profiling persists as an inalienable right in the historical heritage of Liberians. If my notion is an insinuation of that inalienable right then this book will ask two questions; Why is racial profiling based on a belief so thoroughly ingrained in Liberians and; What is it that moves Liberians to act in accordance with the intention of this belief? Most Liberians will not stand up against the purpose of racial profiling as an individual because an identity is closely related to a group, not an individual. Should a Liberian be lured into thinking he or she is innocent of not stopping racial profiling? No.

Liberia is a country where a citizen has to be aware of his or her identity, whether as a descendant of the American black free slaves or a descendant of the African natives. Every citizen will be asked which of the two groups of descendants he or she belongs. This quest for belonging is distinct within family and friends. Where do they get asked and when? In every family, among friends and every neighborhood.

If there is a time for belonging to a certain group, it is when living in a community of Liberians in foreign countries or a particular town in Monrovia. The expectation is readily conceivable that belonging to a group will gain hold on you about racial profiling within the community so you will not leave the community alone.

Sometimes, a person wants to be neutral of not belonging to any group of descendants. But that person will be bothered by family or friends for a choice. Most offspring of intermarriages and interrelationships between descendants of both groups have to choose one over the other. This procedure for identity is a certainty among Liberians.

It could be agreeable by both groups to accept an individual congruence for self identity. But this appreciation of self identity in such an agreement may minimize the potential of each group control of that individual. So individualism is not encouraged as a way out.

Refuting about racial profiling in Liberia is an obnoxious argument when comparing to the preamble of the constitutions of 1847 and 1985. These preambles have provided evidence that racial profiling exists as a problem of ignorance and legality.

When the problem of ignorance and legality becomes a concern for Liberians, the excuse is that the constitution is just about how to govern and who should govern in the political arrangement.

Many readers will find this an unsettling view because Liberians of the past and the present are defenders of their custom, practices, and laws about racial profiling. The many accusatory writings about Liberia have said that racial profiling exists between the two groups who are descendants of American black free slaves and descendants of African natives in the composition of personality.

Today, as in the past, racial profiling weaves together notions of fear and inferiority.

Both of these notions are assumed to be tied to the political arrangement. This awareness of racial profiling is not grounded in genetics or nature but a belief of identity between the two groups. It can be more stringent on both groups to succeed without carrying on racial profiling.

This book about Liberia has two objectors of racial profiling and a perspective that is unique because of equal action in history. The two objectors depicted in this book are descendants of American black free slaves and descendants of African natives on the West coast of Africa. Having considered the ideal of racial profiling, I will show wherein Liberia racial profiling consists.

The first cause for racial profiling in Liberia was the declaration of independence by the American black free slaves and the exclusion of the African natives in 1847. If racial profiling is a pervasive knowledge that assumes the attitudes and values of one group is incompatible to the other group then this is a dilemma for a social condition. There is a fact about interactions, interrelationships, and intermarriages between the two groups in every part of the country. Why is racial profiling still an elusion?

Racial profiling is a fundamental factor that makes Liberians distinctly different from that of other

Africans who were colonized by Europeans. To be a Liberian is an identity of being a descendant of the American black free slaves or a descendant of African natives.

The emphasis for divisiveness is not a disease in the eyes of Liberians to be eliminated, but a condition Liberian lived with and became quite comfortable about as an identity in the realm of belonging.

The second cause for racial profiling in Liberia is the acceptance by the two groups, who want to know for whom Liberia belongs. There have been many wars and many elections as corrective measure for inclusion, but the elusiveness of racialism is used in the political structure by each group. These groups have the responsibility to change the social condition but they are not willing.

The final cause for racial profiling in Liberia is about accountability for the past hatred and the lacking of trust and honesty to build a wholesome functioning country. If the accusation of racial profiling is the divisiveness of Liberians wanting to be in a group then their social condition of existence is unfinished.

Can the reading of the accusatory writings imply that there is existential philosophy in the fabric of Liberians existence? Yes, because existing Liberians do not want to deny that racial profiling is a belief that is incomplete with a limitation like how to use freedom, who have the choice to make that decision, and where does the responsibility come from. This reality of existentialism has permeated alienation, guilt, despair and death on all Liberians since the undetermined event of 1821 to the present. I am saying that existential philosophy is rooted in the discourse narratives of Liberians' historicity.

No doubt the accusatory writings of Liberians and Foreigners about racial profiling have drawn attention to something that is quite fundamental to existing as a core of existential philosophy. Liberians have limited value and are incapable of reaching the understanding for individual thinking.

No doubt the primary function of the offspring from both groups who want to move beyond the belief of racial profiling should tell them as clearly as they can what they are doing and what their particular objective is. Racial profiling is an aim that needs to be stopped as a belief for Liberians. The existence of Liberia is joyful not a dread of social misfits.

1

THE DIVISIVENESS FOR IDENTITY

Liberia holds an historical heritage that sustains racial profiling in the eyes of many people, not Liberians. Why? Because its historical heritage is relating to or based upon the existence of a gun put at the head of an African native chief for land in 1821, which was later called Liberia in 1847 by the American black free slaves. What was the name of this land before 1847? There was none as far as I know because it wasn't colonized.

The use of gun as a force with reason in coercing the African chief was an act of deception and narrow-mindedness. This coercion weaves together the American black free slaves and the African natives into a political system that was separate but not equal for governance. The American black free slaves believe that Liberia should be an exceptional country in Africa for them.

The American black freed-people came to Africa with the help of the American Colonization Society (ACS) in order to forget the deprivation and dehumanization as slaves in the United States of America. With the prospect of self determination to govern themselves, the American black free slaves were willing action against the ACS after the land was given to them.

Since the land was a gift by the ACS to the American black free slaves, it began a centre of feeling. The American black free slaves took the land and guarded it with paternalism. Liberia is a reality by the American black free slaves at last with the intention based on deprivation and dehumanization of the African natives. They knew it was time to stand up for something they truly believed in and made sure to exclude the African natives and requested their independence from the ACS.

Should the action of the American black free slaves about their inheritance be the guide to racial profiling? Yes, because with the help of their faculties, which are fitted to apprehend what is wrong and what is right, is not a definition but an application of racial profiling.

Since I am exploring the transparency of racial profiling, the preamble of both constitutions of Liberia 1847 and 1985 should qualify my assertion that Liberia is a racist nation on the west coast of Africa. The people of Liberia are talking and writing about their ethnic and racial division with clarity but saying they are not racist.

Why do descendants of both groups believe that the love of liberty is the historical heritage of racial profiling? Because such belief of each group sanctifies the illusion about their masquerade of inalienable rights.

It is important to understand the uniqueness of not wanting to be someone else is essential to being who you are. This condition for separate and not equal has an impact on both groups to be hostile and suspicious in the political system. Such forbiddance is an exclusionary rule for a hidden agenda in governance.

This habit to belief in a historical heritage has been a force not to resolve the racial and ethnic conflict that began in 1821. There has been no harmony to govern so war tends to occur between the two groups when power relationships are either unclear or mistaken.

Should the clarification of the accusation of racial profiling between the two groups bring a different result? I don't know if it will. If this accusation is not unique for Liberians then there is no other way to prescribe the attitudes and values of the people.

Where is the historical heritage for racial profiling in Liberia? It is in the attitudes and values of Liberians as an inalienable right. This political culture is no excuse for being marked by an absence of the mind which is held in limits. Its like saying, lets keep this secret to ourselves, as our concern.

My first concern about racial profiling in Liberia is the preamble of both constitutions of Liberia. Preamble of constitution is a statement that usually states the reason for and intent of the law. It is also the facts or circumstances indicating what is to follow.

However, the people of Liberia uphold the preamble of both constitutions in this faction: 1847 for descendants of free slaves and 1985 for descendants of natives.

There is something reliable to proceed with certainty about the historical heritage for racial profiling of each group refusing to debate about their perspective within the preamble of both constitutions. Can a debate led by the groups' offspring for belief in a referendum bring change? I hope so, if the offspring of both groups can avoid paternalism as an identity. Remaining silent about racial profiling is a threat to the dignity of the offspring of both groups.

My second concern about racial profiling in Liberia is the prescription of both groups demanding obligation from Liberians to belong. The task is an obligation for any Liberian to expose the intention of both groups.

Within this obligation there is the assumption as a choice of destiny to clarify the perception of the historical heritage for racial profiling. Should this obligation be wholly a fixation for any Liberian wanting a change in this dysfunctional society? Yes, if any Liberian wants to challenge the belief of racial profiling as an illusion about inheritance.

My perspective that racism as a determinant of human traits and capacities is an astonishing proposal to allow readers into Liberia, my first home. The preamble of both constitutions have created an illusion for a distinct morale of each group as a myth of inherent superiority. It has provided the source of motion, as what something is for, and as the substance of all the people. It is endowed with the authority to subsidy whether the people can grow, be nourished and control the desires of the people for ethnic and racial conflicts.

This justification is the preamble of both constitutions, which is only the indoctrination of all the people regardless of their resistence of being separate but not equal in a political system.

Therefore, the preamble of both constitutions is sanctifying a capability with contrary directions. It is still a problem for me that the preamble of both constitutions is very desirable as the standard historiography of Liberia. So say one, say all, it is the way to be a Liberian.

Constitution, 1847 :

"We the people of the Republic of Liberia were originally the inhabitants of the United States of North America. In some parts of the country, we were debarred by law from all the rights and privileges of men-in other parts, public sentiments, more powerful than law, frowned us down.

Article 1, Section 4- There shall be no slavery within this Republic. Nor shall any citizen of this Republic, or any person resident therein, deal in slaves, either within or without this Republic, direct or indirectly.

Article 4, Section 13- the great object of forming these Colonies, being to provide a home for the dispersed and oppressed children of Africa, and to regenerate and enlighten this benighted continent, none but Negroes or people of Negro descent shall be eligible to citizenship in this Republic."

1985

"We the People of the Republic of Liberia:

Realizing from many experiences during the course of our national existence which culminated in the Revolution of April 12,1980, when our Constitution of July 26,1847 was suspended, that all of our people, irrespective of history, tradition, creed, or ethnic background are of one common body politic.

Article 12- No person shall be held in slavery or forced labor within the Republic, nor shall any citizen of Liberia nor any person resident therein deal in slaves or subject any other person to force labor, debt bondage or peonage, but labor reasonably required in consequence of a court sentence or order conforming to acceptable labor standards, service in the military, work or which forms part of normal civil obligation or service exacted in cases of emergency or calamity threatening the life or well-being of the community shall not be deemed force labor.

Article 27(a)-All persons who, on the coming into force of this Constitution were lawfully citizen of Liberia shall continue to be Liberians citizens. (b)-In order to preserve, foster and maintain the positive Liberian culture values and character, only person who are Negroes or of Negro descent shall be qualify by birth or by naturalization to be citizen of Liberia."

Is there a standard customs, practices, and laws instilled in Liberians for racial profiling? Yes, and it would be bias to say that Liberia is not a racist nation. But my assertion is that Liberia is a racist nation with the preamble of both constitutions for racial profiling in governance and social conditions. A change is necessary to change the current standard.

The purpose for this should not be complex but it is complex in the eyes of the people as descendants of American black free slaves and descendants of African natives who want to strive for a unified country.

Can any change be agreeable for a new condition? The new condition would minimize the continuity of narrow-mindedness by both groups in the mix of racial profiling. However, it is conceivable that both groups have gained their hold on this belief of racial profiling and do not want to vacate the illusion of a historical heritage. The persistence of this illusion had not changed over time since the many wars.

If and only if to say, "we the people have changed evidently," means that each group has acquired certain freedom to inflict harm.

This action of inalienable rights is not an alienation for any group. One may argue that the fear of war again and again as the largest hindrance will not remain silent forever. This fear is loosely identical and tightly identical with both groups.

The important dilemma is merely the direct connection to whose identity will prevail or overcome the illusion of a historical heritage. So the reassurance is to amend both constitutions. This request is clearly the task for Liberians who hope to obtain their prosperity, a society less vicious than the last two centuries.

Is the inheritance for racial profiling in the constitution of 1847 and 1985? Yes. It is those practices built into the ongoing process of the attitudes and values through the intent of the people to exclude. Every Liberian may not be aware of this curse of racial profiling to review it. The reaction of knowing this curse by Liberians is to take action as a choice to debate with ideas, not with guns. The commitment of any Liberian who wants to debate about racial profiling will alleviate themselves from the past and the present reluctance to mention it as a problem. It is refreshing to accept that burden to eliminate this curse as the prerequisite for a responsible condition on an ethical and moral ground. This suggestion may create a resistance from some Liberians because they do not recognize racial profiling as a hollow in the prescription of both groups about the concern to change their habit.

If the foundation of Liberia is the love of liberty then any offspring who is a product of interrelationships or intermarriages between descendants of American black free slaves and the descendants of African natives must prohibit that inheritance called racial profiling. This is the underlining, unquestioning right that reason cannot absolve. All hail Liberia, hail. All hail.

The desire for certitude surfaced in the land that racial profiling is an inheritance from the undetermined events of 1821 as a curse to identify the two groups as Liberians. So the quest for a bulwark of rage is a factor.

2

THE ACCUSATION BY LIBERIANS WRITERS

There is a refutable standing among Liberian writers, which is that the political structure of the past and present should not be based on racial profiling. But they have written historical inquiries which are intone to racial profiling. I explored the writers denial of racial profiling by selecting some of their writings that reiterate my understanding.

Since political system is the process for the convenience of people in a given country to establish a government for the allocation of resources, like opportunities should be the intent and reason for governance.

Can there be a debate about the historical heritage in relationship to racial profiling within Liberia? Yes, but Liberians will not want to debate it.

When I read the preamble of both constitutions, it makes me wonder whether there are still two types of Liberians. We the people are descendants of American black free slaves and descendants of African natives.

For example, obtaining a passport from the Ministry of Foreign Affairs, as a Liberian, in 2013 in Monrovia you were asked which tribe your mother is. This question is not on the official form but is implicitly asked by any officer of the passport division. This act of interjection is distinct and acceptable as a condition to accelerate your chance to obtain a passport.

You have to obligate yourself to the norm of the people as another aspect of the historical heritage to get along in the secret of racial profiling. If I had my way, I wouldn't mention my mother's group.

Since I am a Liberian with the illusion of a historical heritage, I take idleness as the approach not to resolve racial profiling.

Instead, I do what is required of all Liberians, and respond that 'my mother is Kru, a descendant of African natives from Sasstown.'

Can this love of inheritance be an example of racial profiling? Yes, because the attitudes and values of the people will not change. This action is subservience in the historical heritage of racial profiling. The love of inheritance is something which should be understandable as a birth right not a fragmentation and a political structure between the descendants of both groups for obnoxiousness.

This love of inheritance is nothing reliable to proceed with certainty. Such ambiguity for the love of inheritance is also the belief in a habit by Liberians as the only people with an illusion to be racist.

To comprehend this love of inheritance is to be in that moment as a racist Liberian. But Liberians overlook the fact that illusion has essentially two forms: that of hope and that of recollection. Illusion makes Liberian people behave as racist within the concomitance of Liberians.

The historical heritage advocates that reality can be neatly packaged as an interlocking system. This is an illusion of holding the desire and intention together as fulfillment in the eyes of the people.

Should the American black free slaves have privilege over the African natives after the ACS agents gave them the land? No.

I want to make sure that the undetermined events of 1821 should be realized as a matter of chance taken by the ACS agents. Undetermined events are specific conditions not under the control of anything but the opportunity to take action at once. Should the African chief be responsible for giving land to the ACS? Yes, it was the moment for harmony. Could there have been another way without the use of a gun? No.

To be jealous of something that's not for you can bring an emotion of want. If you take an action to acquire that want without the consent of the owner, it can lead to hatred.

This is why there are many sorrows among Liberians, which Bai T. Moore mentioned in his book (Murder In The Cassava Patch, 1968), "Tene, I don't know if the old people ever told you. Kai's father was a shiftless fellow and liked to roam about. His in laws, that is Kai's maternal grandfather and mother, got into some big trouble once.

Rather than suffer humiliation, they sold the poor fellow across the Lofa River and he has not been heard from since. This is a deep secret. Keep it under the roof of your tongue. Kema, there is a lot to learn in this world, isn't there?

"After all I had heard, I did not wish to face the girls. To get drunk was the obvious thing which came to my mind. Tene reached a tall palm tree and put down the rattan basket she had balanced on her head. Sitting in a thicket near the palm tree, my forehead crashed on a stupid twig. Tene heard the frightening sound and looked around. Her eyes caught mine. Softly she said, 'Kai, that's you? Kai.' She screamed."

Before 1821, the African natives were aware of the Europeans intention. Now came the white Americans with a request for land. This was a surprise to the African natives who could not understand the intention of the white Americans about land for the American black free slaves.

The problem begins with the demarcation of the land into individual's property by the American black free slaves. The African natives were astonished that the American black free slaves started to put restrictions on the land, like no trespassing or farming. This was new to the African natives for the use of land to be an individual's property. They had been using land as a community property.

It is more pinpointed by what Ernest Jerome Yancy said in his book (Historical Lights of Liberia's Yesterday and Today, 1967), "Thus, out of this brotherly feeling and sympathetic spirit they gave the pioneers more land. These relationships, however, did not last long between the indigenous tribesmen and the pioneers and their offspring."

If there is no distortion of the fact that American black free slaves are Americans, then their historical heritage is based on racial profiling. To distort is to twist out of the true meaning or proportion of the facts. Liberia is a gift from the ACS.

There are evidences of many actions taken by the United States Government officials to alleviate racial profiling caused by Liberian Government officials against the African natives.

Some actions taken are mentioned by Joseph Saye Guannu in his book (A Short History of the First Liberian Republic, 1985), "With continuous reports pouring into the United States Department of States concerning social and political corruption and human rights violation in Liberia, the Government of Liberia and United States concluded that the League of Nations should inquire into the charges of slaves and forced labor. The League's three-man commission came to be called the Christy Commission. In conclusion, the Christy Commission established that slave trading which involved the selling of human beings was not going on in Liberia but forced labor and pawning of humans actually existed in the country and Liberia Frontier Force used terror and violence to recruit laborers for public work and shipment to Fernando Po."

The allocation of resources in Liberia were not used proportional to improve the well beings of all the people because racial profiling was the function of a pervasive policy.

There was early concern by the African natives about the intention of the American black free slaves excluding them from participation in the decision making of the country. This act of exclusionary rule is merely to say that the historical heritage of racial profiling is paramount in Liberia.

Gabriel I. H. Williams demonstrated the neglect of using all the people in the resources for development in his book (The Heart of Darkness; Account of Liberia's Civil War and it's Destabilizing Effect in West Africa, 2002), "Amid ostentatious display of wealth by the Americo-Liberians or Congos, indigenous Liberians endured poverty and neglect."

If there is a debate on how to build Liberia, it is obvious that the American way is the way to embrace. Every Liberian since 1847 has been mesmerized of being American, not being African.

This pathway of Americanization, not Africanization is more about the historical heritage of racial profiling. But Liberian writers will disagree about this pathway, but agree that it is the Liberians way. One of them in particular is D. Elwood Dunn who explain it in his book (Liberia and Independent Africa, 1940 to 2012; A Brief Political Profile, 2012), "Liberia Rising 2030-The stated objective is to determine a national vision to guide the country's future course of development. This may be the first of its kind since Liberian independence 165 years ago. Doubtless, Liberia's African vocation will figure prominently. Also likely to be highlighted is the relationship between Liberia's unique role in the making of the post-World War 11 African political order and Liberia's post-civil war African aspiration."

Liberians like to be annuitant because they want rewards like payment or positions in government as entitlement without doing anything to achieve it. There is a tendency among Liberians to recognize a person from a family who had ascertained a level of honor. The next of kin or offspring of the former honoree will demand some appreciation and want benefits regardless if the honor was 100 years ago.

Helene Cooper in her book (The House at Sugar Beach; In Search of a lost African Childhood, 2008), reiterates these thoughts. "I was bored. 'Mama Grand,' I said, tell us about Matilda Newport. Oh Matilda Newport was a great woman, she said. 'She whipped those country asses. Bam Bam- blew them all up.'"

The awakening of a desire for revenge has been a circular ingress in Liberia. The problem began after the undetermined events of 1821 by a gun to the head of a Chief for land. The land was taken by the ACS and given to the American black free slaves. When the American black free slaves started utilizing the land with impudence there was resistance from the African natives as well as the agents of the ACS. This attitude of disregard for others transferred into racial profiling, which gradually led to self determination and a request for independence from the ACS, who wanted control.

The awakening of a desire to retaliate for the past crime does not stop. This is crucial for Liberians not to eliminate disparities and not to achieve justice in a society that fulfills the promise for all Liberians. This behavior is documented by Bill Frank Enoanyi in his book (The Trouble With Us; Reflection of a Liberian Journalist, 1990),

"A Colonization Society sponsored the venture, and though an irony of history, the experience of the alien group establishing itself as the overlords of an indigenous group was scarely different from that of other colonial contexts where the alien group happened to be white or of a different racial stock.

"We have not much outgrowth the Founding Fathers' limited vision of nationhood, at least in so far as sharing developmental opportunities with areas outside of Monrovia is concerned."

It is easy to blame someone else when you don't succeed because the opportunity is control by that person. The request for opportunities in Liberia is not a prohibition to be conscious of fair play in the transformation of resources. If an initiation is taken, it will provide revenues for government, profits for company, and wages for employees. The issue of opportunities is tangible and built on the principle of unanimity in every transaction.

Having the resources like 'Iron Ore' without the know-how to develop it for use is a problem. This lacking of know-how is a deficiency in capability. If there is change to come, it must be the role of private business by local entreprenuer to produce the opportunity needed for a market of goods and services.

The availability of manpower in every area of know-how have been misused for jobs in government agencies. The embarrassment for most Liberians is to be given a job they don't qualify for but want to keep.

The standard for performance in a government job is not to show know-how but only the interest as an honorable government official.

To understand the advocacy for government jobs, Yarsuo Weh-Dorliae explains it in his book (Proposition 12 for Decentralized Governance in Liberia; power sharing for peace and progress, 2004), "I propose that Liberia should have a structure of government which, as far as practicable, is decentralized both in law and in fact. I propose that we should reorganize the executive and legislature branches of government in favor of a decentralized government structire in which there is both political power sharing and revenue sharing between the national government and the political subdivisions."

Since archaeologists and anthropologists have provided evidences of people living on the land before the migration of others, this is to suggest that Liberians are refusing the existence of these people. The evidences of these people as African natives had a casual relation to the land. The role of inference and past experience will be important to say that evidence is constituted by environmental artifacts.

The usage of evidences come from knowledge, which are consciously direct or indirect awareness of activities. If there is a knowledge based on racism than this knowledge is not an excuse for the so-called immigrants to deny that there weren't people on the land a long time ago.

The linkage between the evidence and the African natives lies not in the ability to know alone, but in the ability to ask also. This linkage promotes the difference in condition where there are competing interests.

I hope Liberians will stop being refuter of evidences of the people on the land before it was recognized by contemplation that the land was virgin. This is ridiculous. Because many Liberians are not immigrants. The utilization of inference and past experience simultaneously is remembering facts that appears if and only if like ideas and object. Sometimes ignorance can lead to arrogance, which is easily recognized by the customs, practices, and laws and if not checked will become intentional as racial profiling.

Ellen Johnson Sirleaf, (This Child Will be Great; Memoir of a Remarkable life by Africa's First Woman President, 2009), reads "The Liberian motto is 'the love of liberty brought us here.' Liberians are Africans. Those who were there before the settlers came were Africans. And the settlers themselves, though they brought in different values and different cultural understandings, they too were, in crucial ways, African. It was the reason they came home, and, had they embraced that heritage, history might well have recorded a different tale. Instead they tried to dissociate themselves from all that was part of their blood."

The undetermined events of 1821 by agents of the ACS to use force for land was something unconditional, with intensity to seek a way out. If failure is a condition of inability to perform a normal function like assimilation then the American black free slaves were lacking the capabilities.

What has become of Liberia since 1847 and beyond? Liberians are blaming the failure of the political structure on racial profiling as the cause not to develop a reliable social condition in a system to meet the needs and wants of Liberia.

Tarnue Johnson states (Promoting Dialogue and Democracy in Post Conflict Liberia, 2006), "Despite the early optimism shared by the country's founding father, Liberia today can be justifiably characterized as a failed state.

"Thus, the post war cultural situation must transcend the impediments of the old divisions and reified economic and social structures put in place by national rulers who did not understand the finer details and vital influence of culture as determinative in the process of state formation."

In an indefinable way, racial profiling has sustained Liberians the determination and obligation between the two groups not to change. Is there anything else holding Liberians back? Yes, it is fear to confront the belief of racial profiling.

The fictional Story of how healing came to a West African nation is detailed in K-Moses Nagbe's book (A Scream in the Storm, 2004), "Many musical groups charmed ears with Congo and Country national songs, demonstrating for once that in Liberia, it was nothing but sad thinking which split a potentially beautiful nation of a twin culture into cleavages of Congo = 'the sophisticated' (Africans from bondage in America) and Country- 'the native' (native Africans whom those from America met in that spot of Africa). Such sad social toxin!"

Desiring their divisiveness each group acts to intimidate not to assimilate. Such action is losing amicable alignment and promoting group identity. Objectively this action is notable in the book by Wilton Sankawulo, (Sundown At Dawn; A Liberian Odyssey, 2005), "Perhaps the greatest obstacle to progress in Liberia is the historical accident that some of our people were sold into slavery hundreds of years ago. This tragic legacy has created outright hate and mistrust between descendants of the so-called immigrants and the natives.

"But ancestors of the natives experienced slavery, too, although they were never sold to Europeans.

This preoccupation with a phenomenon beyond our control is self-destructive. Are we then to live in the past rather than confront the problems of today? No people can undo their past. They can only use its lessons to build for a better tomorrow."

There are situations in which a child of African natives descent is given to American black free slaves descent to raise. But a child of American black free slaves descent is never given to African natives descent to raise. How is assimilation different than indentured servitude?

A child for assimilation is living with the adopted family and take their name while in the main house alongside with their children. A child for indentured servitude labored long days in difficult condition for little food, live in a shack next to the main house and went to school only in the afernoon when the other children had returned from school. Why is indentured servitude a product of racial profiling? It is bounding a person to work for you or live within your domain and being disregarded of his or her welfare to maintain a comparative lifestyle.

When a child from one group is accepted as a child without racial profiling by the other group, it is a recognition of liberty for reconciliation. To comprehend this way of looking at Liberians is to read more in the book by Dwaboyea E.S. Kandakai (The Village Son, 2001), "It all had started with her decision to go back to her village after twelve years, to see her 'real' parents who lived about two hours walking distance from Ganta.

"However, before she could think of a suitable and calm reply, Neh seized the opportunity to continue. 'You know, I resent the fact that you have to return to those people, the hold they have on you and the fact that you even carry their name. Could you please tell me what's wrong with your own father's name and is it not good enough for you.' She too started yelling, Do you know what I resent? The idea that you are talking about these people like this and you have not even met them. Do you not see that they are responsible for what I am? In fact, what's so important about what name a person really has? If you want my opinion, I think that it is what's a person is that counts rather than whether her name is the most western or the most indigenous.'

"This was the week that Bendu had got to know Nannie's village and a deep tie had been further strengthened by her forster sister's visit with her, even under the peculiar circumstances. Bendu wondered aloud, 'What if you had not come home? We might all be more or less the same people. Now just by your coming home for a short visit we are all changed somehow and for the better I hope."

3

THE ACCUSATION BY FOREIGN WRITERS

The debate among foreign writers is a concern for the allegorical denial of Liberians about racial profiling. This is a sentiment that began nagging foreign writers soon after they saw or read the repeated atrocities of the past and present situations between the two groups for many wars.

I have selected the words of a few writers to allow readers perspective about the attitudes and values of Liberians. I do not want to interpret what is clear. If there is any bias on my part to select these writers, I hold it as a responsibility to be precise about racial profiling in Liberia between the two groups; descendants of American black free slaves and descendants of African natives.

Racial profiling can be a belief of bitter experience breakout of the confines of wishful thinking for a place of norm by a group. Such understanding of racial profiling is a consciousness to which a group behaves to redress the balance of social justice. Well the masquerade for justice by the group after they have gained political power is the opposite of social justice. Racial profiling is factual in Liberia.

Here are some facts in a book by David Lamb, (The Africans, 1987), "For a long time Africans poked fun at Liberia, disparaging it for adopting attitudes and importing values not in keeping with African traditions. But there was one aspects of Liberia no one mocked and that was stability.

"But in killing Tolbert, Doe and his soldier-politicians had merely identified the symptoms of Liberia's discontent. The causes were more demanding than staging a coup, formulating remedies for national illnesses were more complex than shooting government officials bound to telephone poles.

"Freedom, the people learned, did not come from the barrel of a gun. Only one thing seemed certain as a result of the army takeover: Liberia's first coup d'etat would not be its last. Sadly, there is little to suggest that history won't keep repeating itself."

Can it be accepted that the time for a change of government is unpredicted? Yes. But an evolutionary change is a gradual replacement with reliable result than the coming of a revolutionary change for a quick reaction under animosity.

To comprehend some of the useless killing of people that occurs in Liberia is to read the book by Keith B. Richburg (Out of America, a black man confronts Africa, 1998),

"Liberia was supposed to be the most 'Americanized' of African countries, a nation founded in the 1820s by freed American slaves.

"On Christmas Eve in 1989, Charles Taylor and his rebel army invaded Liberia from the neighboring Ivory Coast. September of the next year, Doe was brutally assassinated, the full horror of the execution captured on a videotape for sale on Monrovia streets."

It is a mockery to suggest the African natives waived their rights to govern. The result from political arrangement is the availability of an oath to have a check and balance in the system. There were disagreements when racial profiling eroded the political accommodation and shifted the interest between the two groups.

To what extent is political arrangement reliable in prospect for accountability when racial profiling is a hidden intent? There is none.

Therefore, the action of negligence can be a purpose to delay the importance of political arrangement. This was the factor in Liberia. But not according to David P. Forsythe in his book, (Human Rights and Peace, International and National dimensions, 1993), "In other words, historical tradition, carefully cultivated by the settlers from the earliest days through World War II, nurtured an informal ideology with the central precept that the settler class comprised the legitimate rulers of Liberia. This historical-ideological source of legitimacy came to be shared both by the settlers (with power) and by the most politically aware indigenes (without power).

"Viewed in hindsight, the disintegration of Liberia, once an African model of political stability, into bloody and inconclusive domestic war is reasonably understandable, even though the actual dates of coup and rebellion could not have been predicted with exactitude."

The American black free slaves decided not to be a servitude to the agents of the ACS while in Africa. This indefinable way of choice is mentioned in the book by James Sidbury, (Becoming African in America; Race and Nation in the early black Atlantic, 2009), "As the ACS offered avenue of social mobility for the elite black emigrants, the most vocal residents of the settlers society that emerged in Liberia came increasingly to view themselves as blacks building an American society in Africa, and less as 'Africans' working to raise a diasporic nation.

"The most fundamental issues, however, involved political rights. They had not sailed halfway around the world and taken up the life of pioneers to continue taking order from white people. They had bee promised the chance to participate in building a society that would contribute to ending slavery in the United States, but they seemed instead to be slipping into bondage in Africa. The colony appeared to held toward a persistent violent struggle over control between the Society and the Settlers.

There was an expectation that assimilation should be administered precisely because it is a privilege. This condescending fact was rejected by the African natives when their land given under gun point was declared independent by the American black free slaves. Can assimilation become racial profiling? Yes.

In the book by A. A. Boahen and J. B. Webster (History of West Africa ; The Revolutionary years 1815 to Independence, 1967) explain that, "In 1900, the Monrovia government pursued a policy of assimilating these Africans. In order to become assimilated, Africans had to up their language for English, their traditional religion or Islam for protestant Christianity, their rights in communal land for private ownership and the loyalty to African institutions for loyalty to the Monrovia government.

"Since indirect rule was not economical and since, in any case, it altered African traditional government, it appears unfortunate that the policy of assimilation was not applied throughout the country in the interest of national unity. Under these conditions Africans frequently revolted against Americo-Liberians rule;

there were major revolts among the Grebo and Gola and also the serious Kru revolt of 1915."

Can Liberians allow a disparate voice to be heard without the use of brutal force? No.

Because to make sustainable political choices and embrace possibilities for peaceful coexistence should be based on a practical factor that political arrangement can be a mindful exercise of resiliency. What is wrong with political accommodation in Liberia? Racial profiling.

It is refreshing to read about the indefinable way of racial profiling by Mary H. Moran in her book, (Liberia, the Violence of Democracy, 2006), "Liberia is in many ways a paradoxical place, often cited as the exception to most sweeping generalization about sub-Saharan Africa.

"Following a military coup in 1980, the situation deteriorated into outright war from 1989 to 1996, leading to complete national disruption, foreign occupation, and the deaths of up to 200,000 people, most of them civilians. Even after a brokered peace agreement and internationally supervised elections in 1997, Liberia could not enjoy an end to violence.

"The Liberian national motto, 'The Love of Liberty Brought Us Here,' clearly did not recognize the presence of consequence 'here' before 1822. It is in this light that the writings of Samuel Yede Wallace and his literate Glebo predecessors must be viewed as an act of resistance. But such projects are a strategy for gaining control not only of the past, but of the future as well."

Since the undetermined events of 1821 did not cultivate the African natives into servitude, there has been a problem of racial profiling. The failure to indoctrinate the African natives by the American black free slaves has not worked. It is important to understand that not wanting to be someone else is essential to who you are.

Francis Mitchell puts it this way in his book (Grown Up Liberia, 1945), "It should be noted that all Liberian officials promote forced labor. If my conception is correct, I believe that having a man to work in your home or on your farm so many hours a day, a certain number of days a week, and so many weeks a month, and so many months a year with a home and meals as his only compensation, is, undoubtedly, forced labor.

"On the whole, slavery and forced labor in Liberia will ever continue because the Liberians are too indolent to work for themselves, those of them who are honest are unable to pay servants, those who are in a position to pay are so accustomed to getting something for nothing, that they can't bring themselves to do business in a legal way.

Every law enacted by the Liberian Government is made against the native man, but the pleasure of the

Americo-Liberian. Liberia, you are grown up. Why do you shirk responsibility?"

The accusation by foreign writers says that racial profiling by both groups is a conviction. What can be done to prohibit that certainty of racial profiling into a new belief for an undetermined events of a different result?

Sometimes, the understanding of racial profiling is an intention of complacency. To avoid such complacency is to digest the advice and consent from W.E.B. Dubois, as a warning sign for racism in a magazine, (Liberia, The League and The United States, 1933),

"Liberia is not faultless. She lacks training, experience and thrift. But her chief crime is to be black and poor in a rich, white world; and in precisely that portion of the world where color is ruthlessly exploited as a foundation for American and European wealth. The success of Liberia as a Negro republic would be a blow to the whole colonial slave labor system. Are we starting the United States Army toward Liberia to guarantee the Firestone Company's profit in a falling rubber market or smash another Haiti in the attempt?"

The source of racial profiling is restricted in a local community as a habit that is binding and built on the principle by which to judge with unanimity. Racial profiling can be a belief for fundamental entitlement of a group to promote a bulwark of rage.

An issue of identity is stipulated in both constitutions of Liberia. To display threat and the use of force for identity is merely an expanded version of empowerment by both groups. If there is a pressurization for trade-off in racial profiling then negotiation can be an amicable resolution.

The undetermined events of 1821 should be viewed as a theory that an agreement is binding only so long as circumstances remain as they were or as they were contemplated at the time. Because the undetermined events of 1821 was quite the deprivation of liberty by agents of the ACS with coercion. Liberians should accept the fact that racial profiling is like a public health outbreak of malaria. Any person can get it.

If the undetermined events of 1821 presupposed every decision ever made by Liberia then it should be a salivation for Liberians to uphold the suggestions from Booker T. Washington in his book (Up From Slavery,1901), "I pity from the bottom of my heart any nation or body of people that is so unfortunate as to get entangled in the net of slavery. I have long since ceased to cherish any spirit of bitterness against the Southern white people on account of the enslavement of my race.

"This is so to such an extent that Negroes in this country, who themselves or forefathers went through the school of slavery are constantly returning to Africa as missionary to enlighten those who remained in the fatherland. This I say, not to justify slavery-on the other hand, I condemn it as an institution, as we all know that in America it was established for selfish and financial reasons, and not from a missionary motive-but to call attention to a fact, and to show how Providence so often uses men and institutions to accomplish a purpose."

It's a hard truth but undeniable that no one group, working alone, can do much to advance a wholesome functioning society. Racial profiling is a fiction and must not be valued above the real personalities of all Liberians. That undetermined event of 1821 is just as true today for all Liberians in being part of an enduring and effective movement to stop racial profiling.

4

THE OFFSPRING OF DIVISION

The desire for certitude surfaced in many writings by Liberians and Foreigners about racial profiling, which reflected a widespread understanding that identity may be a problem to build a united country where war and political system are a mess.

If there is another desire for certitude, it is both constitutions of 1847 and 1985 as the avenue preoccupied with maintaining the boundary of both groups as an identity for empowerment.

Is there a myth of racial profiling in Liberia? Yes, the myth of intermarriages and interrelationships between the two groups have produced offspring who are opposing to choose a group. This is a new fear for both groups who are holding onto the past historical heritage as a bulwark of rage.

Why? Because there isn't a choice of choosing whether any of these offspring are reliable for both groups. These mixed Liberians from both groups have reveled in the entrenched paradox that each group identity is the curse from the undetermined events of 1821. The offspring could be a new gift for Liberia.

However, these mixed Liberians will be considered a threat to both constitutions. They may request an amendment. Can the offspring between both groups prohibit the customs, practices, and laws that perpetuated racial profiling? Yes, if all their efforts are directed at the social conditions and not at the political arrangement responsible for behavior shaped by racial profiling.

Some requirements should be to make sure, with motive and intent, that in the presence of consciousness there is no hatred for any group because of paternalism or harassment. This may be a process of innocence and a promise of a secure condition.

Quite obviously the social conditions which fix unequal opportunities for both groups can be traced back to the undetermined events of 1821. The social condition of the presence can be used as a fulfillment to bridge the gap by the offspring.

The inherent tendency of the offspring is a commitment to pursue a social condition of an inalienable right to make a choice of belonging to no specific group. But if there is a choice to make, it must be the offspring to say I belong to both groups. There is no need to invoke justification for both constitutions or a justification for equality by having time to quest for identity.

The offspring should not devote attention on the process of reconciliation between both groups. Why? Because the offspring are a product of interrelationships and intermarriages and are reconciliatory.

In order to challenge reconciliation for any compatible interactions, the offspring must eliminate that illusion of inheritance. Every offspring should stimulate a new myth that it is capable to believe in one identity, not a consequence to have an identity. Hopefully this identity can influence the attitudes and values about birth and where to belong, without intimidation.

Racial profiling is essential to the preservation of both groups, especially for identity, power, and privilege. But it can be considered a masquerade of inheritance to not change the attitudes and values of the people.

The perspective should be to change from the past burden of belonging to a group to belonging to a wholesome functioning country.

Where is the ready-to-live solution for racial profiling in Liberia? The decision of the offspring of both groups to have a choice as an individual. This choice of being an individual is a test of belonging to no group. Can any offspring reject this request? I don't know. It is easy to challenge racial profiling as a burden.

Is there a privilege for the offspring to challenge racial profiling? Yes. I hope it is not to elaborate and defend a privilege which is perceived to be threatened by both groups. This anxiousness of the offspring should not be a claim that they are individualistically obsessed with a choice to change the social conditions only for themselves, but for Liberia.

At the very centre of existence by the offspring is an unresolved tension between both groups with its possibilities and with its restrictions. To endure anxiety is to have the offspring opened to the reality of the social condition and seeing and understanding as is.

I do know that undetermined event of 1821 was the beginning of problems to come.

The land given to the American black free slaves and a constitution to promote a new identity brought animosity and exclusion in the past and the present. What can be done to bring change? Allowing the offspring to be in control of their own destiny.

Liberians have accepted the undetermined events of 1821 as a historical heritage for racial profiling in many wars and many elections without a permanent resolution. Liberians are still arguing about the constitutions 1847 and 1985 with the perspectives of racial profiling. Both constitutions are public policy of a belief that depends on a relationship for give and take in governance, the relationship can be true and false accomplished.

There is evidence that Liberians must enable themselves to tract and document any findings in the formulation of a value system to believe as descendants of American black free slaves and African natives.

This reflection in term of inference amounts to a belief that the accusatory writings by Liberians and foreigners are facts which Liberians do not deny in practice.

Liberia is for all citizens who want to develop the habits for academic education, private work and opportunity to bring changes in the concern of ignorance and legality. Liberia is 167 years old and still waiting to exhale.

Can the words in this book qualify my assertion that Liberia is a bulwark of rage and a place of racial profiling on the West coast of Africa? Yes. The conception of racial profiling mentioned in this book is not based on a theory but a habit that has been inflicted by both groups of Liberians.

My perspective about racial profiling in Liberia is not a hypothesis assumed for the sake of argument in which any of the groups could control attitudes and values. The historical evidences of the undetermined events of 1821 began the problem of racialism.

If there is a proposition to curtail racial profiling then the arrangement for accommodaton will be the ultimate reason of the offspring to instill a new attitude and a new value.

There is a redemption in Liberia waiting half consciously, the coming of the offspring with an inarticulate way of a new belief in a wholesome functioning country.

CONCLUSION

Throughout the accusatory writing of racial profiling among Liberians and Foreigners have dominant thought about whether to exist on the same land is the real cause or excuse for hatred. The accusation that stemmed from the discourse narratives has exalted descendants of American black free slaves at the expense of descendants of African natives.

The undetermined event of 1821 and the subsequent declaration of independence 1847 are evident that Liberia cannot be changed. Such exceptionalism confines to a kind of customs, practices, and law that make Liberians be mindful of their bulwark of rage.

The divisiveness is a dilemma that Liberians lived with and became quite comfortable about. There is no quest for change, just an outflow of fear to have a choice. Since all the interactions, intermarriages, and interrelationships occurred between the two groups, racial profiling stands out at any given moment.

Why is racial profiling based on a belief so thoroughly ingrained in the two groups of Liberians? What is it that moves Liberians to act in accordance with the intention of the belief? Liberians are racist. The fact that racial profiling is a description directed at the possibilities of hatred, not civil rights. This fact is about customary practices and both constitutions of 1847 and 1985 are not purely at the trust of norm. Although racial profiling fulfills each group in many ways, they may well discover that the offspring are anxious to have a choice to choose a new approach for change.

I have devoted mainly to exploring the understanding of racial profiling with reference to the ways in which there is differences by Liberian Writers and Foreigner Writers.

Apologetically, when Liberians are talking about how infrastructures are built in Liberia; is clear in their eyes that roads, hospitals, school buildings, offices of government agencies, buildings for banks and etc are erected on racial lines. I am saying that racial profiling must be stopped and not contain that as a belief of a social condition.

BIBLIOGRAPHY

Boahen, A.A. and J. B. Webster: History of West Africa; The Revolutionary years 1815 to Independence: Praeger Publisher Inc. New York, 1967.

Cooper, Helene: The House at Sugar Beach; In search of a Lost African Childhood: Simon and Schuster, New York, 2008.

Constitution of the Republic of Liberia: Liberian Government Press, 1847 and 1985.

Dubois, W. E. B: Liberia, The League And The United States, Foreign Affairs Magazine, 1933

Dunn, D. Elwood: Liberia and Independent Africa, 1940 to 2012; A Brief Political Profile: Africana Homestead Legacy Publisher, New Jersey, 2012.

Enoanyi, Bill Frank: The Trouble With Us; Reflection of a Liberian Journalist: Monitor Books Publisher, Monrovia, Liberia, 1990.

Forsythe, David P.: Human Rights and Peace; International and National Dimensions: University of Nebraska Press, 1993.

Guannu, Joseph Saye: A Short History of the First Liberian Republic: Star Books, Monrovia, Liberia, 1985,

Johnson, Tarnue: Promoting Dialogue and Democracy in Post Conflict Liberia: Author House Publisher, Indiana, 2006.

Kandakai, E. S. Dwaboyea: The Village Son: Sedco Publishing Ltd. Accra, Ghana, 2001.

Lamb, David: The Africans: Vintage Books, Random House Publisher, New York, 1987.

Mitchell, Francis: Grown Up Liberia: Published in the U.S.A. copyright 1945.

Moore, Bai, T.: Murder in The Cassava Patch: The Anchor Press Ltd, Great Britain, 1968.

Moran, Mary H.: Liberia; The Violence of Democracy: University of Pennsylvania Press, 2006.

Nagbe, K-Moses. : A Scream In The Strom: Author House Publisher, Indiana, 2004.

Richburg, Keith B.: Out of America; A Blackman Confronts Africa: A Harvest Book, Harcourt Brace and Company, Florida, 1998.

Sankawulo, Wilton: Sundown At Down; A Liberian Odyssey: Dusty Spark Publishing, Houston, 2005.

Sidbury, James: Becoming African in America; Race and Nation in the Early Black Atlantic: Oxford University Press, New York, 2009.

Sirleaf, Ellen Johnson: This Child will be Great; Memoir of a Remarkable Life by Africa's First Woman President: Harper Collins Publisher, New York, 2009.

Washington, Booker T: Up From Slavery: Signet Classic Publisher, New York, 1901.

Williams, Gabriel I. H.: Liberia- The Heart of Darkness; Account of Liberia's Civil War and its Destabilizing Effect in West Africa: Trafford Publisher, Canada, 2002.

Weh-Dorliae, Yarsuo: Proposition 12 for Decentralized Governance in Liberia; Power Sharing for Peace and Progress: Bushfire Ventures, LLC, Philadephia, 2004.

Yancy, Ernest Jemore: Historical Lights of Liberia's Yesterday and Today: Around The World Publishing Ltd, Israel, 1962.

ACKNOWLEDGMENT

I am deeply grateful to my six sisters, one brother and two deceased brothers for all the fun during childhood and early adulthood in Liberia. They used to call me "kwi pe ju" in Kru. Thanks to many friends in Liberia and the United States.

I dedicate this book to my mother, Kieh Tih Taplah and foster father, Taplah Boih.

I am overwhelmingly grateful for the vibrant community of teachers who have listened to and agreed or disagreed with me from Kindergarten through High School in Liberia, as well as College. I earned a Bachelor degree in Political Science, 1983 and a Masters degree in Religious Studies, 1985 at Sacred Heart University, Fairfield, Connecticut, U.S.A.

Thanks to my editor, Dawn M. Garcia for reading the manuscript and suggesting rearrangements.

Thanks to the many people who worked with me in Liberia and the United States, especially at Lincoln Industries, Nebraska.

If I'm annoyed by anything it is the reminder that I am part of both groups and racial profiling is paramount among Liberians in Liberia and out of Liberia. I am not ashamed of being a child of a descendant of an America black free slaves from Careysburgh and a descendant of an African native from Sasstown of Liberia.

I am responsible for the contents of this book and no person shall be blamed for how and why it is written about Liberians and Liberia.

Thanks to those who may read this book.